Mad Woman

KAT SAVAGE

ISBN-13: 978-1530327232
ISBN-10: 1530327237

Before You Read This

To put it simply, this one is for me. I had so many doubts while writing and assembling this one. If I said "No one is going to like this" once, I said it a hundred times. Then, a couple of friends reminded me of something very important. They said, "Write for you." So I did.

These are my strange thoughts, my internal conversations. These are snapshots of mad moments and lessons learned in odd ways. I talk about socks and Britney Spears and cutting off my breasts. None of it makes sense. And yet, for me, all of it makes sense. This is my madness.

This is for my sister Angela, who would have turned 27 the day this book released. She was taken too soon. I miss her all the time. The ache is unimaginable. She was one of the maddest women I've ever had the pleasure of knowing and, for that, I am lucky.

If you relate to any of this, you're mad too. And that's amazing. This is for all the mad women. Don't change a damn thing. You are important to me.

Thank you for reading.

I am so delicate

and I need someone to help me

tell my story

I'm Sorry,

I Thought We Were Talking About Me

My two most favorite books are by the same author. He typed them, bound them by hand, and gave them magnificent titles only we would understand. Most pieces have never been seen by anyone but us. I love them because they are about me. Every single word.

And that was when I realized I'm a narcissist.

When I told him this and he asked me, "Does it make me a narcissist too, knowing I wrote your two favorite books?"

I told him yes.

And that was when I realized we are all narcissists trying desperately to forget this long enough to fall in love with each other.

Most love, I've observed, is narcissism at its finest and most cunning. Love is always about how you feel but not necessarily how the other person feels. The notion that simply because you love someone they should be willing to love you in return.

I love you.
Here I am.
Love me back.

And we have the audacity to be wounded over the loss of something we never really had.

They say you can't help who you fall in love with and I suppose that's true. But, as narcissists, we must remember we love ourselves more than we loved them. And we are better than licking our wounded asses in public.

We are better than that.

Acquired Tastes and Retrospect

The first
    "I love you"
will taste like
    hope.

The last
    "I love you"
will taste like
    a lie.

The
    "I love you"
that you waited for
    but never arrived
will taste like
    a blade.

Always Wander, Always Wonder

I pulled my feet across the pavement about as gracefully as a woman feeling terribly aware of her own lack of direction could manage.

I remembered a time when going nowhere was quite all right and even quietly encouraged.

"Take your time," they said.
"Don't rush it," they warned.

And so, I didn't.

But I found the years creep up and if you go nowhere for too long, you will be going nowhere forever, or at least it will feel that way.

I have learned that it's perfectly okay to wander so long as you never stop wondering. You will need it when you finally rest.

Everyone will have questions.

And you,
you will have the answers.

Queen of the Wolves

I have no intention
of kneeling to a man
who isn't willing
to kneel to me.
So if he wants to be a wolf,
I'll let him be a wolf.
He can gnash and claw,
bite and howl.
I'll remind him from time to time
that I eat wolves for breakfast—
bones and all—
and better men have been
on their knees for me, begging.

Queen of the wolves, he calls me.

You have to be a savage to tame one.
But don't misunderstand me.
This has never been about their obedience,
only their willingness to give
what they expect.

So if he wants me to be a wolf too,
I'll be a wolf.
I'll bite and howl,
gnash and claw.
A beast will always want to
love a queen.

So I am a queen, waiting.

What Is Written

He is upset
because I don't write about him.

He doesn't understand
I find it difficult
to write about the things
that make me happy.

I am trying to hold onto it,
and if I write about it,
I will ruin it.

I only write about the things
that have hurt me,
that hurt me now.

And so, I don't write about him.
I hope one day he understands.

When I Ramble About Love, It Makes Sense

I find myself always making my bed just before it's time to sleep again and I wonder for a moment why I bother to make it at all. I think I want to feel a little more present than usual and making my bed puts me in a state of "now." Laundry does this too. *I am here, folding clothes. Clothes I wore last week and clothes I will wear again.* Sometimes this is the only thing reminding me I'm here and time has passed.

My Tinder app sits, quiet. It feels like this little lifeboat sitting in the middle of a pond I forget about more often than I remember. I don't know why I have it. Eventually I will delete it again because it's pointless. It has always been pointless.

I watched Disney's *Maleficent* last night. The story of a fairy who had lovely black wings until the man she loved cut them off. But I sort of appreciate what she became afterward. Hell, I downright admire it. I don't think any one of my lovers cut mine off. Instead, they've each ripped out a handful of feathers as they've gone. Leaving me naked and flightless, remembering each pull. These days, I simply shrug.

I read a horoscope once that was supposed to depict the worst version of yourself. It said all my lovers would only know what I wanted them to. It said if I end up alone in the end, it's by choice. I fear I'm becoming this version of myself. I fear more the fact that I like it. Embracing such truth is an odd thing. It feels like something I've always known but never bothered to speak out loud. It's both foreign and at home on my tongue.

I think I will find love one day. I think it will scare the shit out of me. I'm more frightened that I won't know how to let it in and I will leave like I always do when things feel too intense. I don't mind the hurt but the happy can be taken away and that scares me.

I think I will find love one day. And I will try. I will try to let it in.

If Your Faith Is in a Building, Burn It Down

I used to talk to God sometimes
when it was really quiet in my head,
despite the noise from the open mouths
surrounding me.

I prayed for the boy
I thought I loved in junior high
to love me in return.
He never did.

I prayed to God to save my
one-year-old nephew
who was beaten by
his mother's boyfriend.
He died in the hospital,
head full of bruises and tubes.

I prayed when they said
they'd found my sister's body
that they were wrong
and had mistaken another
tiny blonde girl for her.
They weren't wrong.

I pray and nothing happens.
I pray and nothing happens.
I pray and nothing happens.

Prayer is the mechanism
that has robbed me of my faith.
That doesn't mean I curse it.
I still hope it works for all of you.

Dear Josh

You took my virginity from me when I was 15. You were 17, and I didn't understand the expectations of an almost-man. I wasn't old enough to be doing the things you wanted me to do. To top it off, the real cliché irony was it was prom night and I was wearing a white dress.

You took things from me. You were a taker. I couldn't see it then, but the years collect on me and help me see things more clearly.

I blame you for how I feel about sex. I blame you for my lack of concern. I blame you for thinking sex is love. I blame you for how careless I was with both when I was younger. Fourteen years have gone by and I remember the ache in my chest when you pulled me across the bench seat of your car and forced me on top of you. Sex is not meant to be the demands of one and the compliance of another.

If you love me, you will comply.
If you love me, you will comply.
If you love me, you will comply.

Thank you for teaching me all the lessons I should have never learned at 15.

I love me, and so I will not bow. To anyone.

Regards,
The girl you think you still love

Never the Whole

Today I miss your hands
and the way they caressed
my naked skin.

Tomorrow I will miss your lips
and how, as they pressed
against mine,
all the world went white.

Next week I will miss
the sound of your heartbeat
beneath your skin
when I laid my head
upon your chest.

I miss you in pieces.
Only in pieces.

I choose a different piece
each day
and it's easier to swallow.

I never allow myself
to miss the whole of you.

I wouldn't survive it.
And neither would you.

Dating Frankenstein

I had a dream once that I was dating Frankenstein. I was probably nine years old. We were lying under a tree in early autumn and the leaves were falling all around us. I was wearing a white sundress and smiling. I remember suddenly feeling terrified. I was sobbing as I ran from him. He chased after me and I remember that his face was one of confusion.

I think about all the monsters I've dated since Frankenstein. All the ones I've ran away from, all the ones that have made me cry, all the ones that never bothered to chase after me. I think about the look of confusion on my face each time I was left behind wondering what I had done wrong.

I feel nothing but sadness for the monster that lived inside my dream so long ago. I wish I could hold his hand again and apologize. He's the only one who ever ran after me. He's the only one who was harmless.

Therapy Sessions

Some people take pills
to function.

Some drink
their problems
to numbness.

Others pay those
fancy head doctors
to lie on their couch
and talk to the ceiling.

None of this is wrong
but none of it is for me.

So I pay a guy a little less
to stab me with a needle
over and over again,
leaving behind ink.

I lie very still
listening to the hum
of the gun
and I leave all my issues
in the chair when I get up.

And I am better.

From Grace

I don't remember the fall,
only the scraped knees
and gravel in my hands.

Kick me while I'm down.
I'll still be all right.

From down here
all the clouds look like
marshmallows.

Everyone is human
but no one knows
what it is to be
humane.

Keep passing me by
while I puke up
hard choices
all over the pavement.

I fell so far
but I still know more of
grace
than you.

Handle with Care

Unravel me
the way
you would
a spool
of lace,
careful
not to
split me at
the edges.
In more ways
than my
hardened heart
cares to
admit,
I am so delicate.
And I need
someone
to help me
tell my story.

We all collect

and never really lose

The Loss of Weight and Other Things

This year coupled with the year before it has made me fat. I stand in front of one of those really cruel full length mirrors and pinch at rolls I didn't have a few years ago. I grimace. I don't understand how men touch me let alone fuck me.

Today I didn't eat anything until after 2 p.m. I only ate four things. Not four meals. Four individual things. And that's two more than I wanted to eat. I know what's happening. It always goes like this. I start to hate my body again and it knows. I lose my appetite without really knowing it.

My body begins to shrink. I don't notice it but one day my clothes are sagging and I get to rip into my bottom drawer. The one filled with all my skinny clothes.

I touch my body again in front of the mirror and I know it's smaller but I can't see it. I'm still too big. Always too big. So I'll eat less. Until one day I can fit into the pair of jeans I've desperately held onto for the last five years waiting for this moment.

They fit.
And I am happy.
My eyes are sunken in but I'm smiling.

What a shame.

Obsession

I find
obsession
to be
perfectly
reasonable
so long as
you understand
why you
are obsessed
and know
there is no
difference
between
obsession
and
intense passion.
No one
would
question
a woman
with an
intense passion.
Language
can make
a murderer
a saint,
a victim
deserving,
and a lover
a stranger.

Dear Michael

I'm not sure I have the strength to see you anymore. I haven't seen you in a while but I know when you get back in town, you will call me up and ask me over.

You're a great fuck. We both know that. You know my body with the same attention I want you to know my heart. I know this is too much to ask of you.

You tell me I am one of the only reasons you know you still feel anything. But you are one of the only reasons I am afraid to accept love from anyone.

I have to let you go. I don't know which of us will hurt more.

But I hope it's me.

Love,
Your vehement lady

Sometimes the Boogeyman Is a Little Girl

I think I was maybe seven and she was maybe 14 but she could've been 12. I'm not really sure anymore. We all played house together, me and my sister and her and her sisters. She always made me the wife and she was always the husband. And she was the oldest so she was in charge.

I would pretend to do dishes and she would wrap her arms around me. She would tuck my hair behind my ear and stick her tongue in my mouth. I was only seven so I would stand there with my mouth hanging open.

When we had sleepovers, she'd always lie next to me. She once told me husbands and wives always make love before they go to sleep. She told me to take off my nightgown and so I did because we were just playing a game, and we were both girls anyway and no one really warned me about that.

She cupped her hand over my princess panties and started to rub. She climbed on top of me and pressed her large body against my small body and rocked back and forth. She told me good wives like it and so I lied there very still and made no noise at all.

A couple of years ago I read an article that said sometimes children abuse other children because they themselves are getting abused. And this made me sort of sad. For her. For me. For so many.

I am reminded I must teach my daughter about more than strangers lurking in shadows. I have to make sure she knows the boogeyman will sometimes look a lot like her.

Untitled

I think for a moment
the entire universe
is in a state of flux
all around me
and this is why
I expand
and contract
and my lungs fill
and empty
and my heart
accepts him
and rejects him
all within a matter
of a few moments.
And this is me
blaming the universe
for my flaws,
for my loneliness,
and for
my inability
to stand still
long enough
to be vulnerable.

Teaching My Mother Lessons

My mother is screaming in the next room. She's screaming because we are withholding her prescription medications from her. We will not give them to her because she doesn't take them correctly.

She says sometimes she just doesn't want to be here, doesn't want to be awake. What she really means is if she's high enough she won't remember that my sister is dead and not coming back. She rattles off a dozen names and why she needs them. Names like *cyclobenzaprine*. Muscle relaxer. She has pills for her blood pressure, pain pills, stomach pills, and pills to *"get her head right."*

When I tell her she checked out the day my sister died two years ago and I haven't seen her since, it elicits an emotional response. Her eyes well up and for a moment I think I see a glimpse of the woman she used to be. For a moment, I think she's finally walking back toward us through the fog. This isn't the way I want it, but it will have to do.

She screams and she's gone again.

I have learned two things I need to pass on to her someday if she will ever listen.

1. Addiction has many faces. Sometimes it looks like a mother trying to cope with the loss of her child. There's no back alley deal, no needle, no track marks. There's just sadness and a doctor with a prescription pad ready to embrace you.

2. A person doesn't have to pack a suitcase and kiss you goodbye to leave. Sometimes they will slip away quietly sitting right next to you and you cannot reach them.

Fighting Dirty

He knew exactly what to say,
what promises to make
to cause my ears to perk up
and actually consider his offer.

I wanted to stab him
for knowing what I wanted
and using it against me.

Using a woman's
hope and dreams against her
is like bringing a gun
to a knife fight—

You're going to make
a bigger mess,
and piss everyone off.

Everything Leaves

I drove to the drug store down the street and bought a $12 bottle of wine.

That singer guy said, "you can get addicted to a certain kind of sadness." And I think that's mostly true.

I uncorked my wine and put on a pair of sweatpants. I texted him but he didn't respond.

The next singer guy said, "and love is a satire." And I think that's probably true, too.

Maybe I'm just jaded. I look back on yesterdays when I gave more than I should've and wonder where all the love songs have gone.

I told my friend my bones are tired but what I really meant is that my muscles are so fatigued they are pulling away and I don't blame them for wanting to leave.

Everything leaves.
Even parts of yourself.

202/ *SOS*

I am rounded belly
and thick thighs.
There is an X on the tags
in my clothing
and the bathroom scale
reads 202.
If I stare down long enough,
my vision blurs
and it looks like
SOS.

Men say to me,

"You are too big."
"You'd be prettier if you lost weight."
"I prefer petite women."

I don't have time for conditional love
and the only thing
heavy here is how their words
weigh me down,
anchored to my skin.
They latch onto me
like locks of condemnation.

They took the keys with them.

"Friend" Is a <u>Lonely</u> Word

One day you will tell me you've met someone. You will tell me her name and it will be the single most painful thing I will ever hear. It will be nails on a chalkboard fading to white noise in a land where there are no earplugs.

I will never let you know how every time you talk about her, your face lights up and I feel daggers in my spine. My ears will bleed and I will want to cry.

My stomach will hurt sitting across from the two of you at dinner when she says your name wrong. She doesn't say it like it's the only name she's ever wanted to say. The syllables fall from her mouth like it's just another word.

You'll tuck her hair behind her ear, and I will feel so far away, like I am in the middle of a lake and you are calling my name from the dock through thick fog and a suppressor.

On the sidewalk when we leave, you will hug me and whisper "thank you." I will stop my hands from holding onto you too long. You will kiss my cheek and it will still ache an hour later.

To you, you have just introduced your best friend to your new girlfriend and life is good.

To me, I have just watched the man I love fall in love with someone else. To me, I am still in the middle of the lake, in the middle of the fog, and the chance that I will ever reach the dock where you stand is gone.

All of the "maybes," "what ifs," and "one days" are hanging around me in this fog.

And I, I am just your friend.

Metaphors Are Prettier

Have you ever seen a broken string of pearls fall to a
hardwood floor and bounce all over the place and
scatter from you?

I am discombobulated like that. Just like that.

And no one is scrambling to gather me up because I am
not a pearl necklace.

Metaphors are much prettier than people.

I am a broken pearl necklace.
He is the hardwood floor.
And you are the hands that mend me
even if you don't understand this.

7:19 p.m.

It's Saturday and I'm alone.
Though, there is a small human
sitting beside me so close
I can feel their warmth.
Yes.
I am still alone.

I feel more alone when
I'm around other people
than when I'm actually alone.

I don't go out
because everyone is smiling
and happy
and will want me to be happy,
too.
But I don't have
the strength for that
and no good will come
of surrounding myself
with what I do not feel.

Alone is just another
personality disorder
and self-harm
doesn't always make you bleed.

On Things We Lose

I lost my keys once last night and twice this morning. I lost my virginity but that was nearly half a lifetime ago. Its loss still clings to me. I lost an umbrella on the beach and too many pens to the bottoms of too many bags.

I've lost plenty of men to sunrise and plenty more to apprehension. I even lost one to Neverland but now I call him my Lost Boy and so I'm content.

I talk about what I have lost and nothing of what I have gained. Perhaps because I see them as one and the same.

I read *"nothing is ever lost or can be lost"* and I find a great deal of comfort in those words. Do we ever really lose anything? Or is it somewhere else being exactly where it's meant to be? I didn't lose my lovers. I put them where they were supposed to be, where they needed to be.

I kept a tiny piece for myself, the piece no one else would understand. After all, I lost a piece of myself to each of them and they carry it onward.

And so it goes—
we all collect and never really lose.

I am

painfully aware

my heart is fickle

An Open Apology to All of Them Because I'm Not a Good Person

I hurt you,
and I'm sorry.

It wasn't your place
to pay for the pain
that happened to me
before you.

We do that, don't we?
It's a human thing.

I wish I could say
I'd do it differently,
but I'm probably lying.
That's a human thing, too.

If I hadn't hurt you,
you wouldn't have
overcome all you have.
So, you're welcome.

Remember when I talked
about narcissism?

4 Stable for Wild Men

I know it's getting cold outside because I want to wear socks inside and I never want to do that. Not even when the A/C is running and my feet feel cold to the touch. I don't know why I'm talking about socks. I choose obscure things to talk about when I'm emotional and I feel like I might have something important to say.

This morning I was telling someone about a man who, despite the pain he's caused, I will see next weekend. I will see him next weekend because it will probably be the last time I ever see him. He gives me something I've never been able to explain and I need it one more time.

The person I told didn't understand.
They said,
"You just have a stable of studs, don't you? Aren't you tired?"
And all I could say was,
"No. I don't have a stable of men I ride. I am no one's master."

These men run free. They run far away. They go and come back, go and come back. I am the stable. And I think they return to me when their feet are tired and they need rest. They will not stay. Wild men never stay. I am the stable. Begging them to stay. Begging them to stay away.

Broken Begets Broken

When I finished fucking you, I rolled over and lit a cigarette. In this simple gesture, you read my indifference and began talking. Perhaps it was because we didn't cuddle and I wasn't swooning.

You said something about how you didn't think I cared, and something else about ending this, and then asked if you should stay the night or just go.

"Do what you want, love," wasn't an acceptable answer to you. I wasn't sure what else you wanted me to say. Then you said something about wanting me to open up. *Jesus.* This is that awkward moment when you discover everything and nothing about who I am. I butted out my cigarette and gave you what I could manage.

"Listen, it's nothing against you. I'm just not the settling down type. But you can hold me tonight, if you want to."

You seemed disturbed by this confession but you held me anyway.

I lied there, the little spoon, skin to skin with you and yet so far away. You started to snore. My vison blurred, my face wet with sorrow. I wanted desperately to give you the truth.

I'm a broken woman. I was broken by a broken man. Don't fall in love with me. It's a losing game.

This is my truth. The one I will never give you.

Dear Adam

I had hoped to write one book without you in it. I'm unsuccessful here. February wounds me. It's almost over, but I will feel it even in the heat of August. I cannot escape it.

We got high in your car on the way to a basketball game and I don't like getting high or watching basketball. I thought this would tell you everything I have a difficult time saying.

Sometimes you call me and tell me you miss me but I don't think you understand what you're saying and so I tell you I miss you too, but I mean it in the way you do not.

I've made peace with the fact that you don't know how you feel about me. You told me my hands are tiny but they make you melty.

I hope the hands of the next girl are large and cold and your body doesn't melt under her touch. Yes, I can be bitter.

My love for you is stored in the bottom drawer of my dresser. Next week, February will end. And I will not think of you.

You're the only man it still hurts to write about.

Love,
Your always poet

War Paint

Memories in my marrow
seep out and stain my skin.

The ache is always here,
always falling in line
with the drumming
of my heart.

These scars are my badge;
these bruises are my war paint.

I bleed,
but it doesn't hurt anymore.

I Die, I Survive

I told him I was intrigued.
   "Curiosity killed the Kat," I said.
He said,
   "Well I won't kill you."
I replied,
   "There are many ways in which a person can die."
And I left it at that.

I wanted to say more. I wanted to explain what I meant.
I wanted to tell him about that guy who wrote "we all
fall in love many times but never the same love twice."
We all die many deaths, but never the same death twice.

The girl I was in high school is dead. She's not here.
She overdosed on glass slippers and cross-my-hearts.

The woman who said "I do" with my mouth six years
ago is dead. She's not here. She got drunk on soap box
wine and fell into a well of realization. She drowned in
bad habits.

One night I peered at myself in the mirror of a hole-in-
the-wall bar bathroom while I snorted a bump of
cocaine from my house key. I ran a damp finger over it
and rubbed my gums. She's dead too. She choked on her
own polluted dreams after she hanged herself with his
hide-and-seek smile and took half a bottle of little round
regrets.

People die over and over again all the time.
It's the only way we can survive.

Then I Don't Have to Hide

He said he liked my tits
and my first thought was,

*Sometimes I wish I'd find a lump
right here on the side of my
left breast so I'd have a reason
to cut them off.*

Then I thought to myself,

I think that makes me crazy.

And perhaps it does.

But at least then
I could show
a man those scars
and watch him
run away
without ever having
to let him inside.

At least then
I'd have scars on the
outside
that match
the devastation
on the inside.

Holding Hands with God or Something Like It

We are walking down a dimly lit street. It's a Tuesday so the city is eerily quiet. You make a reference to a post-apocalyptic time for comparison and I giggle.

The streetlights cast obscure shadows against all the sleeping storefronts and barely-awake bars in such a way that it looks like the whole city is yawning.

We are holding hands but I don't know why. Our fingers are intertwined and I think we walk this way simply because it's the way we've always walked.

Tonight you remind me we are not dating, that I am not the one. You use the word "friends" to describe the space between us but my other friends don't kiss me the way you do. You tell me you're this comfortable with me because I'm still at arm's length. I respond calmly, as if this is exactly what every woman wants to hear.

We sit in front of the fountains at Triangle Park surrounded by buildings so tall we feel cradled and the babbling water sounds like a lullaby.

You say to me,
    "It's your turn to talk. Talk to me about water."

And so I recite,
    "Your name echoes in my veins and sometimes it's gentle waves and sometimes it's violent wakes but always it is too loud."

You smile and call me "the always poet."

We stand to leave and you take me by the hand the way you always do. You swing me around, straight into your chest and hug me tightly but perhaps a moment too long because I've drifted away, high on the scent of your collarbone.

As we walk back to your car, I look up trying to find the stars but the city is always too bright even when it's sleeping.

Tonight, I find myself counting all of the broken constellations and name one for each part of you I will miss when I can no longer hold your hand, one for each moment with you that feels like less than at arm's length.

I am still counting.

Blood Tastes Like Pennies and Cold Coffee

When he says he feels bad for hurting me, I remember not to say "it's okay" because I read somewhere this response feeds the subconscious notion that their actions are, in fact, okay. So when he says he's sorry, I make sure I tell him I forgive him. This way he knows what he did is wrong and is something requiring an apology.

The whole thing seems unnecessary. He speaks of his hurting me like it's significant. I hurt before him and I will hurt after him and it's all the same now.

He says he'd like to be friends and of course he would. They always do. They adore me but they're not in love with me. I tell him being friends would be nice and it feels like a razorblade sliding across the tip of my tongue.

There I go again.
I've got to stop cutting myself. I've got to stop bleeding for them. For all of them.

Lonely Mattresses and Gasoline Dreams

It's morning
but the sky is still asleep.
I recoil outstretched limbs,
collect myself from the folds of my bed sheets.
My body becomes
tiny and rounded in the
dip of my mattress just left of the center
where I sleep every night.

I am affected by the absence
of another.
Rather,
I am affected by the presence
of a loneliness
that washes over me
evening after evening.

The dip reminds me.
It cradles me
and it whispers to me,
"Let's burn this lonely mattress
and build a blanket fort
atop the ashes."

I find myself agreeing
until I realize I'm listening to a mattress.
I think about how many steps
it is to the nearest lighter
and decide it's too many.

I fall back asleep because this has become ridiculous
and I dream of gasoline pooling in the dip.
Perhaps I will set fire to it tomorrow.
I will still be lonely but my hands will be warm.

Britney Gave Me Hope

Someone told me coconut milk is good for you, so I went to the store and bought six in hopes that it will kill this cancer in me. And when I say cancer, I mean the ghosts.

Sometimes I think about shaving my head circa 2007 Britney Spears. I think she gets it.

I look at some people and I think, *yeah, they know what's really going on.* And that's the kind of thing that fills me with hope.

When you strip yourself of something people expect, of something they have decided is who you are, you become truly free.

Don't let them take you under. Don't let them decide who you are before you've had the chance to.

Melancholy Is a Little Black Dress

I put on sweatpants and make my way to the kitchen. I pour the last bit of wine I have into a glass and make a mental note to get more tomorrow.

Even when I talk to the people I love the most, I feel disconnected. *Pay attention to me. No, don't.* I'm not comfortable with your eyes so fixed on me. It looks like you're about to love me. If you do, it will be harder to hide.

I know there's something wrong when I find myself Googling the symptoms of depression and wondering how many I have. I always need both hands to count.

I don't think I'm depressed. Though, I think there is a sadness within me. The highs are high. And the lows— the lows are too low.

I wear melancholy like a little black dress.
And no one tells me I should change.

Mad Woman

This morning I came into work smelling like too much sex and not enough sleep but absolutely no regret and so I considered myself fortunate.

Afterward, he said he still liked me and so I shot him dead. What I really mean is I laughed so hard it surely killed him. Or maybe just his spirit.

I don't trust men who are enamored with me. They either don't know I'm a mad woman, or they do and adore me anyway.

In one instance, they don't know me at all. They don't understand what keeps me awake at night. They know nothing of my dreams. They've only seen what is skin deep.

In the other instance, they know too much. They have seen the color of the marrow inside all of my skeletons. They know the dark is more comforting to me than the light. And when I tell them I will hurt them, they hold me tighter.

No good will come from either.

And I am painfully aware my heart is fickle.

The Author

Kat Savage has lived in many places but has yet to find home. She is a single mom of two who spends a lot of time pretending she is a dinosaur and building tents with bed sheets. She holds down a day job but hopes to make writing her living one day. She has love for sushi, coffee, getting tattoos, collecting typewriters and reading good books. She probably loved you in another life, but was broken then, too.

Also by Kat Savage: Learning to Speak
Connect with Kat Savage in all these places:
www.thekatsavage.com
Instagram: @kat.savage
Facebook: facebook.com/katsavagepoetry
Tumblr: katsavagepoetry
Twitter: @thekatsavage
Shop @ katsavagepoetry.etsy.com

The Artist

Ashley Elliott, the cover artist, resides and works out of central Pennsylvania. She is a mixed media artist specializing in acrylic paint on canvas. The painting Ella, featured on the cover, is a 16"x20" acrylic on canvas that Kat fell in love with. Check out her work through her Instagram page @the.great.ashby and shop her work at ashleyelliott.bigcartel.com.

59544961R00035

Made in the USA
Lexington, KY
08 January 2017